Understanding Human Behavior

Basic Principles of Behavioral Psychology

Freudian Trips

Copyright Page

© 2023 by Freudian Trips

All rights reserved. No part of this book may be reproduced in any form or by any electronic or mechanical means, including information storage and retrieval systems, without permission in writing from the publisher, except by a reviewer who may quote brief passages in a review.

This book is a work of non-fiction. Unless otherwise noted, the author and the publisher make no explicit guarantees as to the accuracy of the information contained in this book and will not be held responsible for any errors or omissions.

Published by Omniterra Media Inc

First Edition

Visit the author's website at www.freudiantrips.com

Disclaimer

The views and opinions expressed in this book are those of the author(s) and do not necessarily reflect the official policy or position of any other agency, organization, employer, or company. The contents of this book are for informational and educational purposes only and are not intended to serve as professional advice, diagnosis, or treatment.

The information provided in this book is believed to be accurate and reliable as of the date of publication. However, it may include some errors or inaccuracies, and no warranty or guarantee is provided regarding the accuracy, timeliness, or applicability of the content.

Readers are encouraged to consult with professional philosophers, educators, or other qualified professionals where appropriate for personalized advice. The author(s) and publisher shall not be liable for any loss, damage, or harm caused or alleged to be caused, directly or indirectly, by the information or ideas contained, suggested, or referenced in this book.

By reading this book, the reader acknowledges and agrees that they are solely responsible for how they interpret and apply the information contained herein.

This book may also include references to other works, studies, and sources. These references are provided for further reading and exploration and do not imply endorsement or validation of the specific theories, viewpoints, or interpretations presented in those works.

Chapter 1: Introduction

A. Definition of Behavioral Psychology

Imagine you're training a puppy. When it sits on command, you give it a treat, and the puppy quickly learns to sit whenever you give the command. This simple act of training involves a fascinating field of study known as behavioral psychology.

In essence, behavioral psychology is the study of how our actions and behaviors are influenced by our environment. It delves into understanding why we do what we do, based on the stimuli (or triggers) we encounter and the outcomes or consequences that follow.

B. Significance of Understanding Human Behavior

We all wonder, at some point or another, why we act the way we do. Why do we avoid certain foods, gravitate towards specific music genres, or feel compelled to check our phones every few minutes? The answers to these questions often lie in our past experiences and the rewards or consequences that came with them.

By understanding the principles of behavioral psychology, we can better grasp:

Why habits form and how to change them.

How to motivate ourselves and others.

Why certain advertising strategies are more effective.

And even how to improve education and training methods.

But it's not just about individual behaviors. On a larger scale, understanding human behavior can help societies create more effective policies, build better products, and foster healthier communities.

C. Overview of the Book

This book is your window into the captivating world of behavioral psychology. We'll embark on a journey, starting from the basic principles, like how stimuli lead to specific responses, and work our way through advanced concepts, such as the role cognition plays in our actions.

Here's a sneak peek of what's to come:

Stimulus-Response Principle: Discover how certain triggers can lead to predictable actions.

Reinforcement: Dive into the world of rewards and punishments and see how they shape our decisions.

Punishment: Learn about the ethics and effectiveness of using punishment as a behavior modifier.

Extinction and Shaping: Understand how behaviors can be molded, enhanced, or reduced.

Generalization and Discrimination: Explore how our behaviors adapt or change based on different situations.

Cognition's Role: Delve into the mind to see how our thoughts influence our actions.

Applications: From mental health to education, see behavioral psychology in action.

Ethical Considerations: Tackle the moral implications of behavioral interventions.

Challenges and Controversies: Address the debates and criticisms surrounding the field.

By the end of this book, you'll have a robust understanding of why we act the way we do and how you can use this knowledge in various aspects of your life.

D. Final Thoughts on the Power of Understanding Human Behavior

As we set off on this enlightening journey together, always remember that understanding human behavior is more than just academic knowledge; it's a tool. A tool that can help you make informed decisions, influence positive change, and lead a more fulfilled life. So, buckle up and get ready to dive deep into the intriguing world of behavioral psychology!

Chapter 2: The Stimulus-Response Principle

A. Explanation of the S-R Principle

Let's start with a simple analogy. Imagine you're at home and you hear your doorbell ring. Almost immediately, you think, "Someone's at the door!" and you might even get up to answer it. In this situation, the doorbell ringing is a 'stimulus', and your reaction – thinking someone's at the door and maybe getting up – is the 'response'.

The Stimulus-Response (S-R) Principle is just that: an event or thing (stimulus) prompts a reaction or behavior (response). It's a foundational idea in behavioral psychology, suggesting that much of our behavior is a direct reaction to things happening around us.

B. Ivan Pavlov's Classical Conditioning Experiment

Let's take a trip back in time to meet Ivan Pavlov, a Russian scientist. While he started his work studying the digestive systems of dogs, he stumbled upon a fascinating discovery about behavior.

Pavlov noticed that dogs would start to salivate not only when food was presented to them but also when they saw the lab assistant who usually fed them. Intrigued, he decided to run an experiment. He rang a bell every time before he gave the dogs food. After a while, the dogs began to salivate just at the sound of the bell, even if no food was presented.

What happened here? The bell (stimulus) led to the dogs salivating (response) because they associated the bell with getting food.

C. Real-life examples of S-R in action

Morning Alarms: Every morning, when your alarm goes off (stimulus), you might feel the urge to hit the snooze button or get out of bed (response).

Hot Stove: Ever touched something hot accidentally? The moment your hand feels the heat (stimulus), you quickly pull it away (response).

Favorite Song: When you hear the first few notes of your favorite song on the radio (stimulus), you might immediately feel happy or excited (response).

D. Applications in Behavior Modification

Understanding the S-R Principle is not just about knowing why we do certain things. It's also a powerful tool to change or influence behavior. Here's how:

Education: Teachers might use praise (stimulus) to encourage students to participate more (response).

Training Animals: Much like Pavlov's dogs, trainers might use a whistle or click (stimulus) to get an animal to perform a trick (response).

Therapy: Therapists might help someone who's afraid of spiders by gradually exposing them to images of spiders or real spiders (stimulus) and teaching them relaxation techniques (response) to reduce their fear.

Marketing: Ever noticed how certain commercials might use catchy jingles, attractive images, or emotional stories (stimulus) to make you remember and perhaps buy a product (response)?

As we wrap up this chapter, it's fascinating to realize how many of our daily actions, big or small, are influenced by the world around us. The S-R Principle gives us a glimpse into the predictable nature of behavior and how it can be shaped, changed, or reinforced. As you move forward, think about the stimuli in your life and the responses they trigger. Understanding this dynamic can be the key to making meaningful changes in your life and the lives of those around you.

Chapter 3: Reinforcement

A. Definition of Reinforcement

Imagine you're teaching your dog to fetch a ball. Each time he successfully brings the ball back, you give him praise and a treat. As a result, the dog begins fetching the ball more and more eagerly. This positive feedback loop illustrates the concept of reinforcement.

In behavioral psychology, reinforcement refers to anything that increases the likelihood of a behavioral response. It works by associating a pleasant or unpleasant consequence with a particular behavior. Reinforcement can be positive or negative, as we'll explore shortly.

B. Types of Reinforcement: Positive and Negative

There are two main categories of reinforcement:

Positive reinforcement involves presenting something pleasant after a behavior, thereby making that behavior more likely to occur in the future. Examples include praise, rewards, or treats.

Negative reinforcement also seeks to increase behaviors but does so by removing an unpleasant stimulus instead of adding a pleasant one. For instance, buckling your seatbelt stops the annoying beeping sound in your car.

Both types enhance behaviors, just through different approaches - adding a positive or removing a negative.

C. The Role of Rewards and Punishments

Reinforcement is often confused with reward and punishment, but they have distinct meanings.

Rewards are forms of positive reinforcement. Punishments are intended to decrease behaviors, while reinforcement aims to increase them. Reinforcement also simply associates a consequence rather than judging a behavior as good or bad.

Still, rewards and mild punishments can play a role in effective reinforcement strategies. The key is finding the right balance to shape behaviors.

D. Practical Strategies for Effective Reinforcement

Here are some tips for successfully using reinforcement:

Provide reinforcement consistently and immediately after the desired response. This strengthens the association.

Use diverse reinforcers - different rewards, praise words, etc. This builds interest.

Gradually expect larger accomplishments before providing reinforcement. This shapes more advanced behaviors.

Reinforce small steps toward a larger goal. This enables steady progress.

Consider individual preferences when selecting reinforcers. This tailors effectiveness.

With mindful implementation, reinforcement can successfully help modify behaviors ranging from dog training to human education and beyond!

Chapter 4: Punishment: More Than Just Consequences

A. Understanding Punishment as a Behavior Modifier

Imagine you're learning to play a new instrument, and every time you hit a wrong note, someone gives you a light tap on the hand. Over time, you might find yourself making fewer mistakes, not necessarily because you're mastering the instrument, but because you want to avoid the uncomfortable tap. This is an example of how punishment can influence behavior.

In simple terms, punishment is an outcome or consequence that decreases the likelihood of a behavior happening again. It's like nature's way of saying, "Maybe don't do that again."

B. Positive and Negative Punishment Distinctions

Now, the terms "positive" and "negative" here don't mean "good" and "bad". Instead, they refer to either adding or taking away something to decrease a behavior.

Positive Punishment: This is when something unpleasant is added after a behavior. Think of it like our earlier example of getting a tap on the hand after playing a wrong note.

Negative Punishment: This is when something pleasant or desired is taken away after a behavior. For instance, if a child stays up past their bedtime, they might lose their TV privileges the next day.

C. Ethical Considerations and Limitations of Punishment

While punishment can be effective in certain situations, it's essential to consider its ethical implications and limitations.

Over-reliance: Using punishment too often can lead to fear or anxiety and might not teach the individual a better alternative behavior.

Severity: Harsh punishments can cause physical or emotional harm and can erode trust in relationships.

Effectiveness: Sometimes, punishment doesn't address the root cause of a behavior, making it less effective in the long run.

Ethical Concerns: Especially in settings like therapy or education, it's vital to ensure that punishment is used judiciously and with the individual's best interests in mind.

D. Alternatives to Punishment: Extinction and Reinforcement

If punishment has its drawbacks, are there other ways to modify behavior? Absolutely!

Extinction: This involves removing the rewards or consequences of an unwanted behavior. Let's say a child throws tantrums to get attention. If parents and caregivers stop giving attention during tantrums, the behavior might decrease over time because it no longer serves its purpose.

Reinforcement: Instead of focusing on decreasing unwanted behaviors, reinforcement emphasizes increasing desired behaviors. For example, if a student is often disruptive in class, a teacher might praise and reward them on days when they're attentive and cooperative, encouraging more of that positive behavior.

In conclusion, while punishment can be a tool in behavior modification, it's just one of many strategies available. It's crucial to approach behavior change with empathy, understanding, and a focus on positive growth. As we navigate our relationships, learning environments, and even our personal growth journeys, considering the effects and ethics of punishment can lead to more harmonious and constructive outcomes.

Chapter 5: Extinction

A. The Concept of Extinction in Behavioral Psychology

Imagine you always give your dog a treat when he barks. Over time, the dog starts barking more and more. To decrease this behavior, you stop rewarding the barking. The dog will initially bark intensely, but the barking will eventually diminish without the rewards. This process is called extinction.

In behavioral psychology, extinction refers to the gradual weakening and eventual elimination of a conditioned behavior that occurs when the reinforcer is removed. Since the behavior is no longer "paid off," it becomes less frequent.

B. Understanding Extinction Burst and Spontaneous Recovery

When reinforcement is first removed, an extinction burst often occurs - a temporary increase in the behavior before it drops off. It's like the behavior extinguishes with a bang rather than a whimper.

Spontaneous recovery is also common - the previously extinguished behavior suddenly reemerging for a time. This demonstrates that extinction inhibits behaviors rather than eliminating them completely.

C. Practical Applications of Extinction in Behavior Modification

Extinction is often used to reduce problematic behaviors. Examples include:

Ignoring attention-seeking behaviors to extinguish them.

Removing access to video games to extinguish excessive play.

Stopping reprimanding for swearing to extinguish it.

However, care should be taken with potential aggression or self-harm behaviors during the extinction burst.

D. The Importance of Consistency in Extinction Procedures

The key to effective extinction is absolute consistency. Any instance of reinforcing the behavior, even once, can undermine progress through spontaneous recovery.

It requires diligence to not revert back to the original reinforcers. For example, giving in to a child's tantrum even once resets the extinction process. Consistency until the behaviors are fully extinguished is crucial.

Chapter 6: Shaping: Molding Behavior Step by Step

A. Definition and Purpose of Shaping

Imagine trying to assemble a complex puzzle. Instead of trying to fit all the pieces together at once, you start with the edges, building a frame, and then slowly fill in the middle, piece by piece. This step-by-step approach to completing the puzzle is similar to how "shaping" works in the world of behavior.

Shaping is the process of gradually guiding and rewarding closer and closer approximations to a desired behavior. Think of it as sculpting behavior, molding it little by little until it takes the desired form.

B. B.F. Skinner's Contributions to Shaping Techniques

B.F. Skinner, a renowned psychologist, was like the master sculptor of shaping in behavioral psychology. He introduced many techniques and ideas that laid the foundation for how we understand and apply shaping today.

One of Skinner's famous experiments involved training pigeons. By rewarding them for behaviors that got closer and closer to the desired action, he could get pigeons to turn in circles, push levers, or even play a tiny piano! This showed that complex behaviors could be learned in small, manageable steps.

C. Implementing Shaping in Behavior Therapy and Education

Shaping isn't just for pigeons playing pianos; it's a powerful tool in many settings:

Behavior Therapy: Therapists might use shaping to help individuals overcome fears. For instance, someone afraid of elevators might first be rewarded for just standing near one, then for pressing a button, and eventually for riding it.

Education: Teachers can use shaping to build up a student's skills. If a child struggles with reading, a teacher might first praise them for identifying letters, then for reading words, and eventually for reading full sentences.

D. Hypothetical Case Studies Illustrating the Effectiveness of Shaping

Lucas and the Violin: Lucas wanted to learn the violin but got easily frustrated. His instructor began by praising him for holding the violin correctly, then for playing a single note, and gradually for more complex tasks. Over time, Lucas became proficient and developed a love for the instrument.

Mia's Fear of Water: Mia was terrified of swimming pools. Her therapist started by rewarding her for dipping her toes in, then for standing in the shallow end, and eventually for swimming with assistance. Today, Mia loves splashing around and even joined a swim team.

Classroom Participation: Mr. Smith noticed that Jenny rarely participated in class discussions. He began by praising her for listening attentively, then for sharing small insights, and eventually for engaging in full discussions. Jenny's confidence grew, and she became an active participant.

In the grand mosaic of behavior, shaping allows us to place each tile with precision, creating a beautiful and coherent picture over time. It reminds us that progress is often made in small steps and that with patience, guidance, and positive reinforcement, we can achieve the behaviors and outcomes we desire.

Chapter 7: Generalization and Discrimination

A. Generalization: Transferring Behaviors to Similar Situations

Imagine a child who is scared of dogs. When they encounter a new puppy, they exhibit the same fearful behavior. This transfer of a learned response is called generalization.

In behavioral psychology, generalization refers to responding to different but similar stimuli in the same way. If a behavior is reinforced towards one stimulus, it can generalize to comparable stimuli.

B. Discrimination: Responding Differently to Various Stimuli

Now imagine training the child to approach Labrador retrievers calmly. However, they remain fearful towards German Shepherds. This ability to distinguish between stimuli is called discrimination.

Discrimination in behavioral psychology refers to responding differently to various distinct stimuli. While behaviors may generalize across similar cues, discrimination allows for adaptation to nuances.

C. The Role of Generalization and Discrimination in Phobias

Generalization and discrimination both play a role in phobias.

A phobic response to one object or situation can generalize to analogous scenarios. However, discrimination allows phobias to be circumvented in certain contexts.

Balancing both processes is key to managing maladaptive phobic responses.

D. Techniques for Reducing Generalization and Enhancing Discrimination

Some ways to improve discrimination include:

Gradually introducing subtler distinctions between feared stimuli.

Reinforcing adaptive responses to each new stimulus separately.

Preventing avoidance of generalized stimuli to extinguish maladaptive responses.

Mastering generalization and discrimination allows behavior to be fine-tuned to situational nuances.

Chapter 8: The Mind Behind the Behavior: Understanding the Role of Cognition

A. Integrating Cognitive Processes with Behavioral Psychology

Imagine you're at the edge of a diving board, staring down at the pool below. Your heart races, not just because of the height, but because of the thoughts running through your mind: "What if I make a fool of myself?" "Will it hurt?" "Can I do this?" These thoughts, or cognitions, play a huge role in determining whether you'll take the leap or climb back down.

While behavioral psychology focuses on how external factors shape our actions, cognitive processes hone in on our internal thoughts, beliefs, and perceptions. Together, they provide a more complete picture, helping us understand that behavior isn't just about external rewards or punishments, but also about what's happening inside our heads.

B. Cognitive-Behavioral Therapy: Theory and Practice

Merging the worlds of behavior and cognition gave birth to a powerful therapeutic approach: Cognitive-Behavioral Therapy (CBT). In simple terms, CBT is like a two-pronged strategy:

Cognitive: Recognize and challenge unhelpful thoughts. For example, instead of thinking, "I'll never be good at this," you might learn to think, "I'll do the best I can, and that's okay."

Behavioral: Change behaviors that result from or reinforce negative thoughts. If you're afraid of public speaking and avoid it, a therapist might help you face this fear in manageable steps, proving to yourself that you can handle it.

C. Cognitive Strategies for Behavior Change and Self-Management

Harnessing the power of our thoughts can lead to meaningful change. Here are some strategies rooted in cognitive principles:

Positive Self-talk: Replace negative or self-defeating thoughts with encouraging and realistic ones.

Visualization: Imagine yourself succeeding or handling a situation well, boosting confidence and motivation.

Mindfulness and Meditation: Stay present, reducing anxiety and enhancing focus.

Problem-solving: Instead of feeling overwhelmed by challenges, break them down into smaller, manageable parts and tackle them one by one.

D. Challenges and Criticisms of Cognitive-Behavioral Approaches

No approach is without its critics, and CBT is no exception:

Over-Simplification: Some argue that CBT oversimplifies complex emotions and experiences.

Short-Term Focus: Critics point out that while CBT can offer quick results, it might not address deeper, long-standing issues.

Over-Reliance on the Individual: Placing too much emphasis on changing thoughts might downplay external factors that contribute to a person's struggles.

In wrapping up this chapter, it's clear that understanding behavior requires looking both outside and in. While the world around us shapes our actions, the world inside our minds gives those actions meaning, direction, and depth. By appreciating the interplay between behavior and cognition, we unlock a richer, more nuanced understanding of the human experience.

Chapter 9: Applications of Behavioral Psychology

A. Behavioral Interventions in Mental Health

Behavioral psychology principles are widely used in mental health. For example, systematic desensitization utilizes gradual exposure to extinguish phobic responses. Self-management strategies based on reinforcement help reduce addictive behaviors. Cognitive-behavioral therapy aims to reframe thoughts impacting emotions.

Overall, behavioral techniques in clinical settings seek to replace maladaptive responses with more adaptive coping strategies.

B. Behavior Modification in Educational Settings

Educational settings harness behavioral psychology extensively. Positive reinforcement is used to encourage student participation. Modeling desirable student behavior can prompt peers to imitate it. Self-monitoring helps students track their own progress and self-reinforce.

Applied behavior analysis also assesses how factors in the environment influence academic performance to devise targeted interventions.

C. Behavioral Principles in Parenting and Family Dynamics

Many parenting techniques rely on behavioral strategies:

Providing praise and rewards for positive behaviors

Using ignore and timeout for negative behaviors

Setting up clear expectations and consistency

Shaping complex skills through incremental steps

Understanding behavioral principles allows parents to effectively socialize children's conduct.

D. Behavioral Strategies for Personal Growth and Self-Improvement

We can apply behavioral psychology principles to our own lives too. Self-reinforcement can help instill productive habits. Creating motivational associations and environmental cues can promote follow-through. Exposure therapy can reduce anxieties. Gradual implementation of new routines can lead to lasting change.

Harnessing our own human psychology empowers self-improvement.

Chapter 10: Navigating the Moral Compass: Ethics in Behavioral Psychology

A. Balancing Ethics and Effectiveness in Behavior Modification

Let's start with a simple scenario. Imagine you're teaching a child to tie their shoes. Would it be effective to offer them their favorite candy every time they made an attempt? Probably, yes. But would it be ethical to use candy as a reward in the long run? Maybe not, especially if it leads to unhealthy eating habits.

This scenario highlights a crucial balance in behavioral psychology: the line between what works (effectiveness) and what's right (ethics). While certain methods might yield quick results, it's essential to consider their broader implications on an individual's well-being, dignity, and rights.

B. Informed Consent and Autonomy in Behavioral Interventions

Imagine going to a restaurant and being served a dish you didn't order. You'd probably be upset, right? Similarly, in behavioral interventions, it's crucial that individuals know what they're "ordering."

Informed consent means that before any behavioral intervention, individuals should be:

Fully informed about what the intervention involves.

Aware of potential risks and benefits.

Given the choice to participate or not.

This ensures that people remain in control of decisions about their lives, preserving their autonomy and dignity.

C. Addressing Ethical Issues in Research and Practice

Behavioral psychology, like all sciences, relies on research. But delving into the human mind and behavior comes with its set of ethical responsibilities:

Privacy and Confidentiality: Participants' identities and personal information must be kept private.

Voluntary Participation: No one should be forced or unduly influenced to participate in a study.

Harm Avoidance: Research should never harm participants, either physically or emotionally.

Transparency: Researchers should be honest about their intentions, methods, and the potential use of their findings.

D. Future Directions for Ethical Standards in Behavioral Psychology

The field of behavioral psychology, like society itself, is ever-evolving. As we advance, it's vital to ensure our ethical compass also evolves. This might mean:

Regularly Updating Guidelines: As we learn and grow, ethical standards should be revisited and refined.

Inclusive Ethical Reviews: Diverse voices and perspectives should be included in discussions about ethics to ensure a holistic approach.

Public Engagement: By involving the public in discussions about behavioral research and interventions, we can ensure that ethical standards align with societal values and needs.

Closing our chapter, it's clear that while the quest to understand and influence behavior is exciting, it's equally crucial to tread this path with respect, empathy, and integrity. Ethics in behavioral psychology isn't just about rules; it's about upholding the fundamental values that make us human.

Chapter 11: Challenges and Controversies in Behavioral Psychology

A. Debates over Free Will and Determinism

Some criticize that behavioral psychology implies our actions are predetermined, challenging notions of free will. However, human behavior is quite complex. While influenced by prior conditioning, humans can also make thoughtful choices. The degree of free will versus determinism in behavior continues to be debated.

B. The Nature-Nurture Debate in Behaviorism

Behavioral psychology has also been critiqued for focusing too much on external influences while minimizing biological and innate factors that shape personalities and behaviors. However, the interactive effects of both nature and nurture are important for a comprehensive understanding of human psychology.

C. Addressing Criticisms and Advancing the Field

While early behavioral approaches had some limitations, the field has progressed substantially. Modern behavioral science integrates internal mental processes, complex social dynamics, neurological bases, and more. Sophisticated models continue to evolve our understanding of the multitude of factors that motivate human behavior.

D. The Future of Behavioral Psychology in Modern Science

Far from an obsolete science, behavioral psychology remains highly relevant. Its principles are increasingly applied in diverse fields from behavioral economics to digital design. Big data and neuroscience are illuminating new dimensions of behavior. However, the meaningful integration of multiple disciplines will be key to advancing behavioral science in the modern era.

Chapter 12: Wrapping Up Our Journey: The Power of Understanding Behavior

A. Recapitulation of Key Principles

Our journey through the world of behavioral psychology has been enlightening, to say the least. Let's take a brief stroll down memory lane:

We began by understanding that behavior is influenced by both external factors, like rewards and punishments, and internal processes like thoughts and beliefs.

We delved into the mechanisms that drive our actions, such as the Stimulus-Response Principle and the impact of reinforcement and punishment.

We appreciated the role of cognition in shaping our behaviors and the therapeutic approaches that integrate both external and internal influences.

Throughout, we were reminded of the ethical considerations that ensure our understanding and application of behavioral psychology respects human dignity and rights.

B. Empowering Readers with Behavioral Psychology Knowledge

With the insights you've gained, you're now equipped to view the world and your interactions in a new light. You have the tools to:

Understand why people act the way they do.

Foster positive changes in yourself and others.

Approach challenges with a combination of empathy and strategy.

C. Encouraging Further Exploration and Application

Our exploration has just scratched the surface. The world of behavioral psychology is vast, and its applications are myriad. If your curiosity has been piqued:

Delve deeper into specific topics that intrigued you.

Seek out courses or workshops that offer hands-on experiences.

Apply what you've learned in your daily life, whether it's in personal relationships, at work, or in personal growth pursuits.

D. Final Thoughts on the Power of Understanding Human Behavior

As we close this chapter and the book, reflect on the incredible tapestry of human behavior. Each thread, each color represents actions, decisions, and experiences shaped by a dance between the world around us and the world within.

By understanding the principles of behavioral psychology, we don't just gain academic knowledge. We unlock a deeper understanding of ourselves and others, fostering connections, empathy, and positive change.

Thank you for embarking on this journey. May the insights you've gained illuminate your path, helping you navigate the intricate, beautiful maze of human behavior.

About Freudian Trips

Welcome to Freudian Trips, your dedicated platform for diving deep into the world of psychology. We are more than just a YouTube channel or a book publisher. We are a beacon of enlightenment, making complex psychological concepts accessible and engaging for all.

Our YouTube channel is a rich repository of psychology made simple. We take the profound and often complex ideas from the world of psychology and break them down into digestible, easy-to-understand content. From the foundational theories of Freud to the cognitive insights of Piaget, we cover a broad spectrum of psychological schools and thoughts, making psychology accessible to everyone, regardless of their background or prior knowledge.

As a book publisher, we take the same approach, transforming intricate psychological theories into comprehensible narratives. Our books are not just collections of words, but vessels of wisdom that make psychology approachable and relatable. We believe that psychology should not be confined to academic circles, but should be available to all who seek to understand the human mind and behavior.

At Freudian Trips, we believe in the power of curiosity and the pursuit of knowledge. We are here to stoke the fires of your curiosity, to guide you on your intellectual journey, and to help you navigate the fascinating world of psychology.

If you are someone who is not afraid to question, to explore, and to learn, then you are in the right place. Join us on this journey of exploration, as we make psychology easy to understand, one concept at a time.

Be sure to visit our Youtube channel at: www.freudiantrips.com/youtube

You can also visit us on the web at www.freudiantrips.com

Welcome to The Freudian Trip community. Stay curious. Stay enlightened.

www.ingramcontent.com/pod-product-compliance
Lightning Source LLC
Chambersburg PA
CBHW070749260726
48660CB00007B/3035